Contents

You and Your Bones

Imagine yourself with no bones at all—no backbone or leg bones to hold you up, no skull or ribs to cover your soft insides. You'd be a big, pulsating blob, stuck in the same spot for the rest of your life!

The bones of your skeleton give you shape and support. They keep your brain, heart, lungs, and other fragile organs from getting bounced around and bruised. And they team up with your muscles to help you move. Just to take one small step forward, about 200 muscles are needed to move your leg bones, shift your balance and steady your body so you won't fall over. And they're not working alone. Blood cells are busy delivering food and oxygen for en-

X-rays can "see" through your skin to the bones inside; otherwise, your skeleton is invisible!

ergy, and the brain is transmitting detailed directions on when and how to move. Whether you're sitting still or running at full speed, every part of your body has a specific assignment—and

Every time you stand up or sit down, chew your food, or even listen to your favorite music, your bones are on the job—without any direct orders from you!

all the parts must work together to keep you alive and well.

This book will introduce you to your own skeleton and explain how it works with the rest of your body. You'll discover how you react to the outside world, how you move, and how you think. You'll find projects to do, either on your own or with a "skeleton crew" of friends, as well as Body Watch boxes that describe your body's built-in safety measures. You'll learn what happens to food after it's chewed and swallowed, how you "shrink" during the day and "grow" again at night, and why you yawn, hiccup and get goose bumps.

This is a guide to your body—make no bones about it!

LIFE WITHOUT BONES

The first forms of animal life, three billion years ago, had no backbones in their small, simple bodies. Today their backbone-less descendants, called invertebrates, include insects and worms, starfish and jellyfish—members of a group that comprises over 97% of the animals on our planet. Insects alone outnumber human beings by a staggering ratio of 200 million to one!

Boning Up

The bones that come with this book fit together to form an accurate model of an adult human skeleton. Just pop the bones into place, and move them individually to see how your own skeleton works.

When not in use, the model can stay on display in its own see-through case.

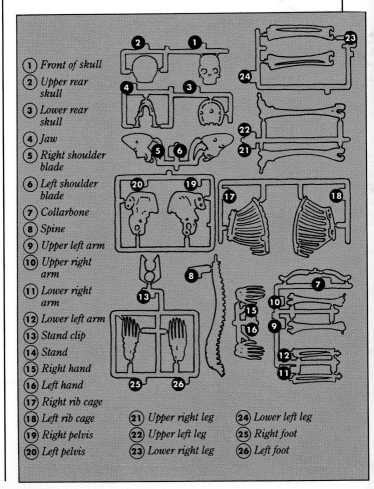

1. Front of skull
2. Upper rear skull
3. Lower rear skull
4. Jaw
5. Right shoulder blade
6. Left shoulder blade
7. Collarbone
8. Spine
9. Upper left arm
10. Upper right arm
11. Lower right arm
12. Lower left arm
13. Stand clip
14. Stand
15. Right hand
16. Left hand
17. Right rib cage
18. Left rib cage
19. Right pelvis
20. Left pelvis
21. Upper right leg
22. Upper left leg
23. Lower right leg
24. Lower left leg
25. Right foot
26. Left foot

A. *Right rib cage* 17 *into spine* 8 *. Left rib cage* 18 *into spine* 8 *.*

B. *Right pelvis* 19 *into spine* 8 *. Left pelvis* 20 *into spine* 8 *.*

C. *Upper right leg* 21 *into lower right leg* 23 *; right foot* 25 *into assembled right leg. Upper left leg* 22 *into lower left leg* 24 *; left foot* 26 *into assembled left leg. Assembled right leg into right pelvis* 19 *. Assembled left leg into left pelvis* 20 *.*

D. *Lower rear skull* ③ *into upper rear skull* ②. *Front of skull* ① *into assembled rear skull. Jaw* ④ *into assembled skull. Assembled skull into spine* ⑧.

E. *Right shoulder blade* ⑤ *into right rib cage* ⑰. *Left shoulder blade* ⑥ *into left rib cage* ⑱. *Collarbone* ⑦ *into rib cage* ⑰ *and* ⑱. *Upper right arm* ⑩ *into lower right arm* ⑪; *right hand* ⑮ *into assembled right arm. Upper left arm* ⑨ *into lower left arm* ⑫; *left hand* ⑯ *into assembled left arm. Assembled left arm into left shoulder blade* ⑥. *Assembled right arm into right shoulder blade* ⑤. *Stand clip* ⑬ *into rib cage* ⑰ *and* ⑱. *Stand* ⑭ *into clip* ⑬.

Make sure you know your left foot from your right! When the skeleton is facing you, its left side will appear to be on the right—and vice versa.

Bone Directory

Forehead
(Frontal bone)

Nose bones
(Nasals)

Cheek bone
(Zygoma)

Upper jaw
(Maxilla)

Lower jaw
(Mandible)

Collarbone
(Clavicle)

Breastbone
(Sternum)

Upper arm bone
(Humerus)

Lesser forearm bone
(Ulna)

Main forearm bone
(Radius)

Thigh bone
(Femur)

Kneecap
(Patella)

Main shinbone
(Tibia)

Calf bone
(Fibula)

Ankle bones
(Tarsals)

Foot bones
(Metatarsals)

Toe bones
(Phalanges)

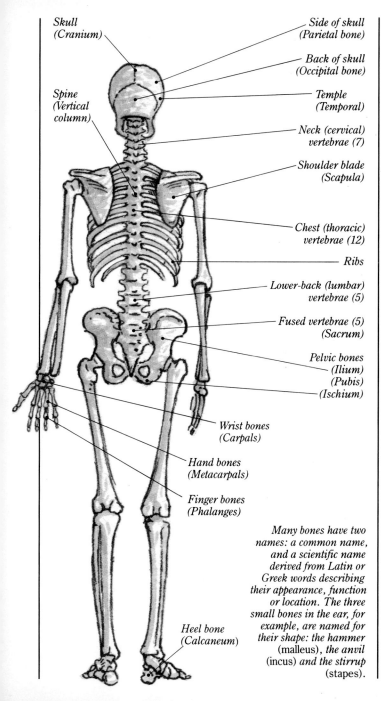

Skull
(Cranium)

Spine
(Vertical
column)

Side of skull
(Parietal bone)

Back of skull
(Occipital bone)

Temple
(Temporal)

Neck (cervical)
vertebrae (7)

Shoulder blade
(Scapula)

Chest (thoracic)
vertebrae (12)

Ribs

Lower-back (lumbar)
vertebrae (5)

Fused vertebrae (5)
(Sacrum)

Pelvic bones
(Ilium)
(Pubis)
(Ischium)

Wrist bones
(Carpals)

Hand bones
(Metacarpals)

Finger bones
(Phalanges)

Heel bone
(Calcaneum)

Many bones have two names: a common name, and a scientific name derived from Latin or Greek words describing their appearance, function or location. The three small bones in the ear, for example, are named for their shape: the hammer (malleus), *the anvil* (incus) *and the stirrup* (stapes).

Bone Basics

Y̲ou may not realize it, but your bones are alive and growing inside you. Tiny bone-building cells are constantly at work, shaping your skeleton from one day to the next. First come the osteoblasts, which cruise along the bones' growth surfaces and build layers of a protein material called collagen. Then particles of the mineral calcium phosphate get stuck in the collagen and crystallize to form new bone.

Much of this growth is taking place in the gap between the shaft and the end of each bone. By the

Fifty percent of a bone's weight comes from minerals. A third of each bone is protein, and the rest is mostly water.

Most growth in the long bones of the arms and legs occurs in the cartilage that separates the end from the shaft.

Blood vessels

Spongy bone

The longest bone in your body, and perhaps the strongest, is the thigh bone (pictured here). Its long shaft is a tube with outside walls of very thick, solid bone to withstand all the bending, twisting and impact forces caused by your active life.

time your skeleton reaches adult size, around age 20 or so, all the tough, milk-colored cartilage that fills the gap will have turned to bone.

While your bones are growing, your skeleton not only gets bigger but also changes its proportions. When you were only a few days old, for example, your head was as big around as your chest and about a quarter the length of your body. When you reach

Small pores, or holes, leading from the outside into the interior, allow blood vessels through to nourish the bone and carry away wastes.

Marrow

Dense outer layer of compact bone

VANISHING BONES

In your lifetime, you'll "lose" about 600 bones! Before you were born, your skeleton contained over 800 separate bones, many of which grew or fused together so that you had about 450 at birth. By age 20, when your bones have finished growing and the separate parts have joined together, they'll number only about 206.

CURIOUS CARTILAGE

Long before you were born, your skeleton was made completely of cartilage—the same rubbery substance you see at the fat end of a chicken "drumstick." Gradually, the temporary cartilage hardened and became bone. Some cartilage, however, such as the wiggly end of your nose and the outer part of your ear, is permanent and will never harden into bone. This type is also found in the disks between the vertebrae of your spine and at the ends of bones where they meet at a joint.

In old age, the disk cartilage shrinks, but some permanent cartilage grows larger—and may cause your ears and nose to grow!

adulthood, your head will be half as big around as your chest and only about one-seventh of your body length!

THE WONDER OF BONES

How can bones be strong enough to carry your weight, yet light enough not to slow you down? Bones get their amazing strength from calcium, phosphorus and other minerals—some of the same minerals found in rocks. And your skeleton doesn't feel heavy because all the long bones are hollow!

Still, this doesn't mean that bones are empty. In the otherwise hollow interior of many bones is a substance called marrow, which manufactures most of your blood cells. Without these cells, the rest of the cells in your body would wither and die.

CELLS:
The Body's Building Blocks

Visible only through a microscope, cells are the smallest units of the living tissues that make up your body structure. Different types of cells, each with separate assignments, form specific kinds of tissue. Bone cells clump together to make bone tissue; muscle cells, whose function is to move the bones, create the muscle tissue that actually does the job.

Nerve cell

Muscle cells

Cells are always dividing in two to make more cells. Some new cells add to your overall growth, while others serve as replacements for the three billion cells that die every minute. Body cells also get bigger. When you reach adulthood, your heart will be 16 times larger than when you first came into the world, but it will have precisely the same number of cells.

Just think—your life began as a single cell, the fertilized egg in your mother's body, and in just about 40 weeks you grew to become a human being!

Red blood cell

White blood cell

15

Muscle Power

Without muscles attached to your skeleton, you'd be stuck in one place like a useless "bag of bones"—doing nothing and going nowhere! Every single part of your body has muscles, working nonstop to keep you lively and on the go.

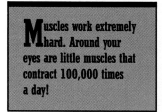

Muscles work extremely hard. Around your eyes are little muscles that contract 100,000 times a day!

Some 650 muscles cover your skeleton to hold your bones in place and make them move. Attached at both ends by tough cords of tissue called tendons, these skeletal muscles work in pairs to pull the bones into position. You can observe your muscles at work by placing your left hand on the large biceps muscle of your upper right arm as you bend the arm into a "strongman" pose. The muscle will bulge as it shortens, or contracts, to pull up your forearm. Under your right arm is the relaxed triceps muscle. Straight-

The long, thin fibers of skeletal, or voluntary, muscles are laid out in rows side by side and contract more rapidly than other muscle fibers.

MUSCLE SENSE

Electrical signals from the muscles let your brain know your position at all times. Thanks to this "muscle sense," you can cross a room without looking down to make sure that one foot is properly placed in front of the other.

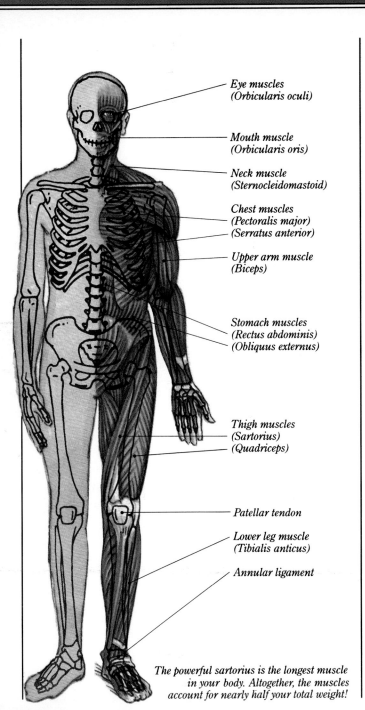

Eye muscles
(Orbicularis oculi)

Mouth muscle
(Orbicularis oris)

Neck muscle
(Sternocleidomastoid)

Chest muscles
(Pectoralis major)
(Serratus anterior)

Upper arm muscle
(Biceps)

Stomach muscles
(Rectus abdominis)
(Obliquus externus)

Thigh muscles
(Sartorius)
(Quadriceps)

Patellar tendon

Lower leg muscle
(Tibialis anticus)

Annular ligament

*The powerful sartorius is the longest muscle
in your body. Altogether, the muscles
account for nearly half your total weight!*

en your arm, and feel the biceps relax, or lengthen, as the triceps tightens to pull your forearm down.

Contractions of skeletal muscles are started by electrical signals from the brain, and the strength of each contraction depends on the number of signals. For example, you use the same muscles whether you pick up a brick or a pencil, but when you pick up the brick there might be 50 times as many signals!

INDEPENDENT MUSCLES

Skeletal muscles work *voluntarily*, which means they follow commands from your brain, but other muscles are beyond your conscious control. These smooth, *involuntary* muscles line the internal

Upper back muscle
(Trapezius)

Shoulder muscle
(Deltoid)

Upper arm muscle
(Triceps)

Back muscles
(Infraspinatus)
(Latissimus dorsi)

Buttock muscles
(Gluteus medius)
(Gluteus maximus)

Hamstring muscles
(Biceps femoris)
(Semitendinosus)
(Semimembranosus)

Calf muscle
(Gastronemius)

Achilles tendon

With all our human strength, we can never match the real musclemen of the animal world. Most insects can lift 20 times their own weight!

organs such as the stomach, blood vessels and lungs. Operating on their own, day and night, involuntary muscles push food through your digestive tract, keep your blood circulating and enable you to breathe—all without any thought on your part.

The heart muscle has a different structure, but luckily you don't have to remember to make it beat, either!

Powerful cardiac muscle fibers form the wall of the heart. These small, often branched fibers attach end to end.

The fibers of smooth, or involuntary, muscles cross over each other to allow stretching or contracting in two different directions.

FEEL IT IN YOUR BONES

To demonstrate the benefit of using your muscles as levers, try lifting a brick two different ways. First, hold your arm out straight, grip the brick from the top and raise it in the air without bending your elbow. Difficult, isn't it?

Using the bones as levers, opposite muscle pairs such as the biceps and triceps alternately contract and relax to bend or straighten the arm.

Now, without changing your grip, turn the brick over so that it rests in your palm and pull it up toward your shoulder as you bend your arm. This way is easier because your muscles worked on the "lever principle," pulling against the bone.

PICKUP AND DELIVERY:

The Circulatory System at Work

Fresh from the bone marrow, new red and white blood cells pass into the bloodstream and begin their journey through the 60,000-mile (96,500-kilometer) network known as the circulatory system.

Floating in a pale fluid called plasma, the red cells pick up oxygen from the lungs and little bits of food from the digestive tract and deliver them as fuel for the rest of the body's cells. The far less numerous white cells patrol the bloodstream to fight infection by attacking germs.

FEEL IT IN YOUR BONES

Measure your own heartbeat by placing your fingertips on the pulse at the inside of your wrist, about three finger-widths from the base of the thumb toward the elbow. (Be sure not to use your thumb, which has a pulse of its own.) You'll feel blood being pumped through your wrist on its way to your hand at a rate of approximately 72 to 75 beats per minute when your body is at rest. Women have slightly higher heart rates than men. Athletes of both sexes can have much lower resting heart rates—down to about 50 beats per minute!—because exercise has trained their hearts to deliver a higher volume of blood with each beat.

Jugular vein

Heart

Carotid artery

Red blood cells get their color from hemoglobin, a pigment molecule that attracts and carries oxygen and carbon dioxide. Lacking hemoglobin, most insect blood has a yellow or greenish tint.

Aorta

Upper branches of lungs

Axillary artery

Subclavian vein

Inferior vena cava

Iliac artery

Iliac vein

Femoral artery

Some major arteries and veins of the circulatory system. (Arteries are shown in red; veins, in blue.)

The power center of the circulatory system is the heart, beating day and night inside the rib cage to pump blood through the arteries, veins and capillaries. A little larger than your fist, the heart receives blood from the veins and sends it to the lungs for oxygen. Bright red, oxygenated blood returns to the heart and is pumped out through smaller and smaller arteries until it enters the capillaries, whose thin walls permit food bits and oxygen to pass right through to the body cells.

Blood cells line up single file to pass through the narrowest capillaries.

Meanwhile, in the opposite direction, wastes squeeze into the bloodstream through the capillary walls to be carried in veins to the organs that dispose of them. Carbon dioxide, for example, is taken to the lungs and expelled from your body every time you breathe out; other wastes are processed in the kidneys and liver.

It seems like a long journey, with many tasks along the way, but one round trip through the circulatory system takes only about 60 seconds—and the cells make the trip about 1,400 times a day!

TO THE RESCUE!

When you cut your finger or scrape your knee, white cells in the vicinity move in and "chew up" any invading germs. Broken bits of blood cells called platelets, originating in bone marrow, also go to work at the emergency site by clumping together to seal off the broken blood vessels. Clotting, or coagu-

Your body's repair team races to the site of a cut. Platelets clump together to form a plug, while white blood cells cruise the bloodstream to attack bacteria and other invaders.

lation, takes place when chemicals from the platelets combine with other substances in the blood and form a scab over the cut or scrape.

THE HEART OF THE MATTER

Pulmonary veins

Left atrium (receives blood from the lungs via the pulmonary veins)

Valve separating atrium from ventricle

Right atrium (receives blood from the body through the superior and inferior vena cava)

Heart muscle

Two pumps in the heart work side by side to keep blood circulating. The right-hand pump forces oxygen-spent blood to the lungs, while the left-hand pump squeezes oxygen-rich blood out to the rest of the body through the arteries.

Each pump has two chambers: an atrium and a ventricle. As blood travels from one to the other, small valves open and shut to keep it on course. What you hear when you listen to your heartbeat is the sound of these valves slamming shut.

Aorta

Pulmonary artery

Left ventricle (pushes blood out to the body's tissues through the aorta)

Right ventricle (pushes blood out to the lungs through the pulmonary artery)

The heart is made of the strongest muscle in your body. In one year, it beats almost 40 million times.

The Skull and Sensory Organs

The human skull appears to be one large, rounded bone with a separate piece for the lower jaw, but in reality it consists of 29 different bones! Fifteen are found in the jigsaw puzzle of the face, where sockets protect the eyes, nosebones guard air openings, and upper and lower jaw bones encase the tongue and teeth. Six small bones deep within the skull are used in hearing (see page 25). And the eight thick bones that form the cranium, the major part of the skull behind the face, safeguard the brain from hard knocks.

Babies are born with gaps between their skull bones, leaving soft spots covered by skin. For the

Frontal bone (forehead)

Parietal bone

Temporal bone

Nasal bone

Zygoma (cheekbone)

Maxilla (upper jaw)

Mandible (lower jaw)

Your "solid" skull is made up of many parts— 28 plus the lower jaw.

Semicircular canals

Malleus (hammer)

Incus (anvil)

Stapes (stirrup)

Eustachian tube

Deep inside your skull, at the end of the ear canals, are the six smallest bones in your body. Vibrations set up in these bones allow you to hear!

first few months, before the bones grow together, you can see the largest soft spot beating at the top of a baby's head as blood is pumped to the brain!

NOT JUST FOR CHEWING

Rooted in the spongy bone of your jaws, your teeth are used for biting and grinding food, giving shape to your face, and making certain speech sounds. The first teeth to come in are the "baby teeth" (or "milk teeth"), which number 20 in all by age 2. Starting about age 5 or 6, these are gradually replaced by a permanent set that will total 32 by age 18—when the "wisdom" teeth erupt through the gums. The crown of each tooth is covered by shiny white enamel, the hardest material in your body.

"Baby tooth," about to be replaced by a permanent tooth

Enamel

Dentin

Gum

Jaw bone

25

THE HUMAN ANTENNAE

Sight. Visual information is first received in the form of light rays, which the lens of your eye focuses as upside-down, reverse images on the retina. Receptor cells, called rods and cones, in the retina change these "light pictures" into electrical signals and feed the information to your brain, which "sees" it in its original form.

Retina

Optic nerve

Lens

Iris

Pupil

SIGHT

Nerves to brain

Hearing. Traveling into the wide funnel of your outer ear, sound waves reach your brain through a series of vibrations that begin in the eardrum. This thin piece of skin causes the hammer bone to vibrate and hit the anvil, which activates the stirrup to set up vibrations in the fluid of your inner ear. Nerve endings located here send electrical impulses to your brain, which interprets them so that you can recognize your mother's voice, for example, or tell the difference between the bark of a dog and the song of a bird.

Supporting cells

Olfactory cells

SMELL

Smell. Odor molecules—from fresh-baked cookies, let's say—enter your nose and brush against a hidden organ called the olfactory mucous membrane. Receptor cells in the membrane send information to your brain, which recognizes this particular combination of molecules as the smell of cookies.

Taste. Distinguishing one taste from another requires a cooperative effort between your tongue *and*

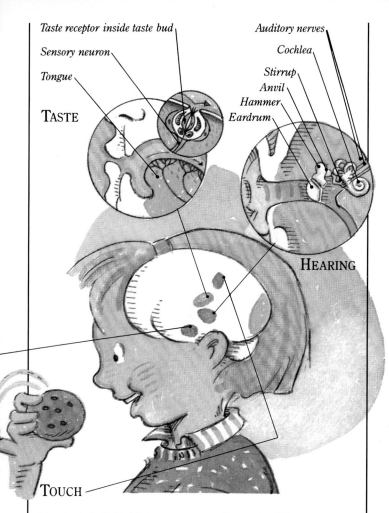

TASTE

Taste receptor inside taste bud

Sensory neuron

Tongue

Auditory nerves

Cochlea

Stirrup

Anvil

Hammer

Eardrum

HEARING

TOUCH

Your brain is divided into separate areas that receive different sensations from the nerves, as well as areas for the control of movement and other functions.

your nose. Taste buds on your tongue tell you whether food is sweet, salty, bitter, sour—or just plain awful. Without the odors transmitted by your nose, however, food would have no flavor at all.

Touch. Information received from touch, the only sense not located within the skull, is transmitted by nerves spread over the skin.

27

THE MESSAGE CENTER:

The Miraculous Brain

W orking quietly inside the skull, the brain sorts through an infinite stream of messages from the five senses, stores important information in its memory bank, and takes action when necessary by setting the appropriate muscles in motion. Most thinking is done in the cerebrum, the largest and busiest part of the brain. The left half, or hemisphere, of the cerebrum is responsible for

Impulses travel from the axon of one neuron to the dendrites of another in less than 1/10,000 of a second.

TRAINING THE BRAIN

E very time you learn a new activity, electrical impulses blaze a new path from one motor neuron to another and your brain has to memorize this new pattern of connections. Sometimes, especially if the new activity involves many muscles moving simultaneously, you might have to repeat the movements many times until they're clearly recorded on your mental videotape. That's why learning to ride a bicycle usually requires several tries before it becomes "second nature."

speech and intellectual activities; the right half controls creativity and emotions. A communications system connects the two, so that one side always knows what the other is doing.

Cerebrum

Anger, fear and other feelings are believed to begin in the hypothalamus, also known as "the seat of emotions."

Physical coordination is handled by the cerebellum.

Sensory messages to the brain are sorted in the thalamus and routed to the proper receiving centers.

Spinal cord

THE NEURON EXPRESS

Safeguarded by covering membranes and cushioned by fluid, the brain owes its efficiency to billions of delicate nerve cells called neurons. Each neuron picks up impulses through small fibers called dendrites and passes them on through the axon, a long, single fiber that "connects" with the dendrites of other neurons.

Even though the brain accounts for only 2% of your body weight, 20% of all your energy goes into the billions of connections that occur every second within its nerve tissue. Without these connections, you couldn't think, move, feel—or remember your own name. In fact, you wouldn't be alive!

Each tiny neuron is a transmitter cell that runs on your own chemically fueled electrical system

29

THE GREAT CONNECTORS:
The Spine and Spinal Cord

The skull sits on the spine, a snake-like column of 25 separate bones called vertebrae. Also known as the backbone, this column supports your body and protects the spinal cord from injury and disease. Like the links of a bicycle chain, each vertebra allows a little movement so that the spine as a whole enjoys a great deal of flexibility.

The curve of the spine reduces strain on the muscles and allows you to keep your center of gravity over your legs and feet. No matter how loudly someone tells you to "straighten up," you could never straighten your spine all the way.

At the top of the spinal column, the *atlas* vertebra swivels on the *axis* directly beneath it, thus allow-

HELP, I'M SHRINKING!

Believe it or not, you're taller in the morning than at night. Measuring your height against a door frame first thing in the morning, and again in the early evening, will prove that you've lost about a quarter of an inch (half a centimeter) during the day! Gravity and your own daytime activity have compressed the cartilage pads, or disks, between the vertebrae in your spine, causing it to shrink. Don't worry, though: when you're asleep, the cartilage absorbs water from your body and puffs up again.

ing you to move your head. The *thoracic* vertebrae each match up with a pair of ribs; the *lumbar* vertebrae carry the weight of your upper body and anchor the heavy muscles of your lower back; and the five fused vertebrae that form the *sacrum* lock the base of the spine to the pelvis.

The final four vertebrae are fused together to form the *coccyx*, or "tailbone." If you had a tail, this is where it would attach!

Brain

Axis
(2nd neck
vertebra)

Atlas
(1st neck
vertebra)

7 neck vertebrae

Nerves

12 thoracic vertebrae

Your brain weighs only three pounds (1.4 kilograms) but contains 50 to 100 billion nerve cells! Because these cells work so intensively, your brain uses up 20% of your body's oxygen.

5 lumbar
vertebrae

Sacrum

Coccyx

The giraffe's neck, the longest in the animal kingdom, has only seven vertebrae—just like yours.

Some snakes have more than 400 vertebrae, each with its matching pair of ribs.

TWO-WAY COMMUNICATIONS

Running through the canal formed by the vertebrae, the spinal cord links your brain with the rest of your body. About three-quarters of an inch (two centimeters) thick, this "nerve trunk" begins with the brain stem, which controls the involuntary muscles used in unconscious actions such as breathing and digestion, and extends all the way down to the first lumbar vertebra. Branching out from the cord are 31 pairs of nerves, each dividing into smaller nerves so that every part of your body can communicate with your brain.

The vast network of nerve cells formed by the spinal cord and brain is known as the central nervous system. Through individual neurons in the nerves, *sensory* information is carried from your body to your brain while *motor* commands are relayed from your brain to your muscles. Neurons extending from the lower part of your spinal cord to your toes can grow to four feet (1.2 meters) in length!

BODY WATCH

Sometimes the nervous system uses shortcuts to speed up reaction time. If you touch a hot stove, for example, nerves in your hand might send an *"Ouch, it's hot!"* message to your spinal cord, which will immediately send back its own signal: *"Then move your hand!"* The microseconds saved by these unconscious "automatic reflexes" can prevent serious injury.

FEEL IT IN YOUR BONES

Brain

Spinal cord

Recruit a friend to help you demonstrate the "kick reflex." Cross one leg over the other at the knee—and relax. Have your friend tap the gap between your kneecap and shinbone with a toy hammer or with stiffened fingers. What happens? Each time your friend taps, the tendons connecting your kneecap to your upper leg bones and muscles jerk your lower leg forward as your thigh and calf muscles contract. This kick reflex is "ordered" by nerve connections from your spinal cord.

Cauda equina ("horsetail")

The spinal cord relays information to and from your brain and controls automatic functions such as breathing.

Sciatic nerve

Nerves

Every once in a while, you'll feel a mysterious muscle contraction in your eyelid or cheek. These sudden contractions, or tics, can be caused by "misfires" of nerve signals when you're very tired or under stress.

33

ALL SYSTEMS GO!

Picture someone tossing you a ball high in the air. Your brain, acting on information from your eyes, follows the ball, estimates its size, and calculates its speed and height as it begins to drop. Simultaneously, messages from your brain to your muscles let you reach toward the ball, stretch, and finally close your hands around it at exactly the right instant. It's only a simple game of catch, but imagine how many computers it would take to control and direct a robot to do that—and to smile after the ball is caught.

The incredible organic computer inside your skull can send electrical signals along some of your body's longer nerves at 300 miles (480 kilometers) per hour. No wonder your reaction time is so fast!

"IN WITH THE GOOD, OUT WITH THE BAD":

The Rib Cage and Respiration

Strong, lightweight and flexible, the rib cage backs up the chest muscles as protection for the lungs, heart, liver and stomach, as well as some of the major blood vessels.

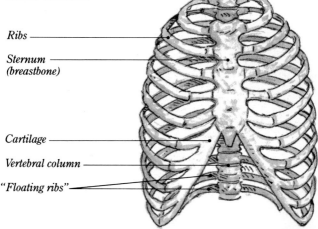

Ribs

Sternum (breastbone)

Cartilage

Vertebral column

"Floating ribs"

FEEL IT IN YOUR BONES

Lean back in a chair, take a deep breath, and feel the shape of your rib cage and the point where your ribs attach to the sternum, or breastbone. The top of this bone is the notch at the base of your throat between the two collarbones.

Although all 12 pairs of ribs are attached to the thoracic vertebrae, only the first seven connect with the sternum, or breastbone. The next three pairs attach to cartilage at the ends of the other ribs. The last two pairs, called "floating" ribs, are held in place only by muscle tissue and do not attach in front.

The ribs can move slightly at the point where they attach to vertebrae and to cartilage in front of the rib cage. Ligaments and muscles between the ribs lift and separate them to allow the lungs to expand. Every time you breathe, your ribs have to move!

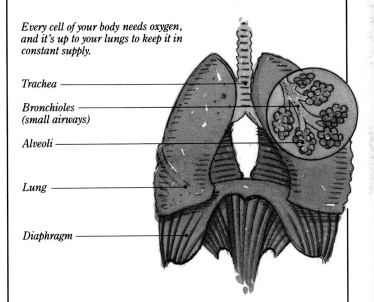

Every cell of your body needs oxygen, and it's up to your lungs to keep it in constant supply.

Trachea

Bronchioles (small airways)

Alveoli

Lung

Diaphragm

THE LUNGS...

The respiratory system is responsible for bringing oxygen into your body and releasing waste in the form of carbon dioxide gas. As you breathe in and out, air travels to and from the lungs through a long tube called the trachea. Suspended like long oval sponges within the rib cage, the two lungs are made of an elastic material that allows them to expand. Inside are

37

clusters of little balloon-like sacs called alveoli, which receive the air through small tubes in the lungs. Believe it or not, several hundred *million* of these tiny air sacs fill up and empty 15,000 times a day! Oxygen from the air passes through the thin alveolar walls into capillaries, where red blood cells pick it up and carry it to the heart for distribution to the rest of your body.

In exchange for the oxygen, the alveoli receive carbon dioxide from the capillaries. Carbon dioxide, which is waste from the breakdown and use of food by your body, is eliminated when you exhale.

... AND HOW YOU BREATHE

The work of the lungs relies on the chest muscles and on the diaphragm, a thick sheet of muscle stretching across the bottom of the chest cavity. As the chest muscles lift the ribs, the diaphragm contracts and pulls downward, giving the lungs more room. The lungs expand in the wider space, and new (or "good") air rushes in to fill the slight vacuum created by the drop in air pressure. When the muscles relax, the air pressure rises, the lungs deflate, and used

BODY WATCH

Your body has thought of everything! Even the hairs in your nose are there to catch dust and other undesirable particles that might otherwise find their way to your throat and lungs. Smaller particles that sneak past this first line of defense are swept in a sticky mucus to your nose and mouth, where you can expel them by coughing, blowing your nose, or sneezing. *Atchoo!* Away go the irritating particles, sometimes at hurricane force—nearly 100 miles (160 kilometers) an hour!

FULL OF HOT AIR!

To see how much air your lungs can hold, you'll need a large plastic jug, a rubber or plastic tube, a marker—and a friend. Fill the jug with water, then fill the sink halfway. Have your friend place one hand over the top of the jug, turn it upside down and hold it underwater in the sink. Then insert one end of the tube underwater into the neck of the jug. Take a deep breath, place the other end of the tube in your mouth, and blow out as long as you can. The air exhaled from your lungs will displace the water.

Turn the jug right side up and mark the water level, then fill it up again and switch places with your friend. Whose lungs hold the most air? For an exact answer, use a measuring cup to fill the jug up to the marks.

("bad") air is forced out through the nose and mouth.

You can control your own respiration whenever you decide to take a deep breath, or "blow it all out," but normally the muscles contract and relax on their own to regulate your air supply. When your breathing rate slows down, the diaphragm will even force a wide yawn to take in more air.

Sometimes the diaphragm contracts unexpectedly, causing a case of hiccups. A sudden rush of air strikes the covering flap of the "voicebox," making the vocal cords move and resulting in a series of *hics* that can last for hours!

YOUR OWN FOOD PROCESSOR:
The Digestive System

The digestive system changes what you eat into fuel for your cells and rids your body of everything it can't use. Since you probably eat about half a ton of food each year, this system works overtime!

Digestion starts in the mouth, where saliva softens food as you chew. Small pieces and liquids then squeeze through the esophagus into the stomach, a bag-like organ shaped like the letter "J." Here, juices and enzymes break them down into even smaller bits while muscles in the stomach walls churn them into a soupy mixture called chyme. It may take you 20 minutes to eat dinner, but your stomach needs at least three hours to process the food.

TASTE TEST

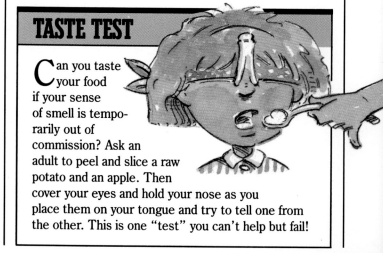

Can you taste your food if your sense of smell is temporarily out of commission? Ask an adult to peel and slice a raw potato and an apple. Then cover your eyes and hold your nose as you place them on your tongue and try to tell one from the other. This is one "test" you can't help but fail!

Esophagus

Liver

Made of elastic material,
the stomach can stretch to
twice its size while fitting
its shape to the food inside.
When food leaves the
stomach, it shrinks back
to its normal size.

Gallbladder

Pancreas

Large intestine

Small intestine

Anus

*The digestive tube, also known as the alimentary canal,
starts in the mouth and ends at the anus—reaching a length
of 30 feet (9 meters) in the adult body.*

41

Muscle contractions force the chyme into the small intestine, where capillaries pick up the nutrients for distribution throughout the body. (The small intestine is only "small" in diameter; stretched out, it would reach about 21 feet, or 6.5 meters!) Next, the large intestine (only 5 feet, or 1.5 meters, long) takes the "leftovers," removes the fluid, and passes the waste out through the anus at the end of the line.

DIGESTIVE AIDS

Also at work in the digestive process are two organs that leak their contents into the small intestine. The liver, curved up under the diaphragm, pours acid bile into the intestine; the pancreas, behind the stomach, secretes additional enzymes. The liver is especially helpful in breaking down fat into nutrients that the body can easily use.

The two bean-shaped kidneys, found below the rib cage and behind the intestines on either side of the spinal column, contribute to digestion by regulating fluids and salt in the body and ridding the blood of wastes, which pass to the bladder in the form of urine. Working surprisingly hard for their size, the kidneys filter 425 gallons (1.6 milliliters) of blood each day!

THE ALL-PURPOSE TONGUE

Many sets of muscles, running in different directions, give your tongue an extraordinary amount of versatility. You use it for tasting food, for making separate sounds when you speak, and also for swallowing. The base of your tongue, far down your throat, is attached to the hyoid bone—a U-shaped bone that is loosely connected to the base of your skull and forms a link to your trachea and esophagus.

BODY WATCH

Directly in front of the esophagus is the trachea, or breathing tube. When you're ready to swallow a mouthful of food, the trachea knows to close the epiglottis—a little "trap door" behind the tongue. If a mix-up occurs, and food enters the trachea by mistake, choking is the uncomfortable consequence.

Swallowed food passes into a 10-inch pipe called the esophagus. The pipe's muscles squeeze each mouthful of food and push it through a "door" that opens to let it pass into the stomach.

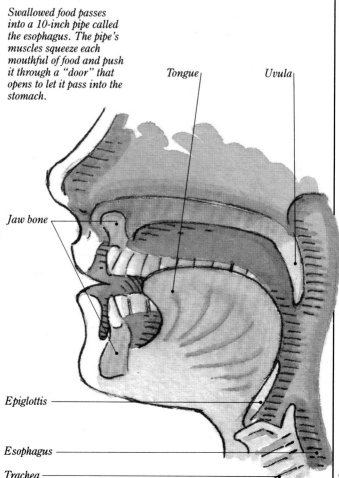

Tongue

Uvula

Jaw bone

Epiglottis

Esophagus

Trachea

A GOOD LOOK AT YOUR LIMBS:
The Arms and Legs

The arms and legs are the most visible parts of the body, yet it's hard not to take them for granted. After all, they seem to move by themselves, providing balance and support as if they had minds of their own.

You probably never noticed the many similarities between your arms and legs, an inheritance from the early human ancestors who walked on all fours. Both sets of limbs begin at the top with one large bone, attached to the body with the same kind of joint (pages 48–50). And each lower limb has two separate bones, connected to the upper limb by a similar joint.

FEEL IT IN YOUR BONES

It's easy to touch the ends of your lower arm and leg bones. You can feel the top of the ulna as the large, jutting point of your elbow and its bottom end as a knob at the outside of your wrist. At the base of your thumb, on the near side of the wrist, is the bottom of the radius. Similarly, at the outside of your ankle, you can feel the knobby end of the fibula (what we call the ankle bone); at the inside of the ankle is the end of the tibia.

Unlike the bones whose main job is to protect your organs, the arm and leg bones are used chiefly for leverage and locomotion. These bones allow the arms to swing from the shoulders, while the legs swing from the hips.

Has your leg or foot ever "fallen asleep"? This happens after you've been sitting with your legs crossed, with one leg pressing on a nerve (and sometimes a blood vessel) in the other leg and preventing its signals from getting to your brain. When you change position and release the pressure, the nerve signals suddenly flood your brain and you feel the sensation known as "pins and needles."

45

Of course, there are obvious differences, too, in their size and the jobs they do. Your arms are smaller than your legs, with weaker muscles, because they don't have to support your whole body and move you along. On the other hand, fewer muscles are needed in your legs because less flexibility is required of them.

Also, unlike the lower leg bones, the radius and ulna in the lower arm are nearly the same size and can swivel over each other when you want to turn the palm of your hand up or down. In the leg, the large tibia, or shinbone, contributes more support than the thin fibula and is very sensitive to bumps because of its nearness to the skin.

The kneecap has no counterpart in the arm. What we call the "funny bone" in the elbow is actually a nerve running over the end of the ulna behind the humerus. A bump on this nerve can send a tingling shock all the way down to your fingers!

NATURE'S KNEE GUARD

About the same size as the "pocket" of your palm, the kneecap bone, or patella, is not connected directly to the other leg bones but instead is embedded in large tendons in front of the knee. From this vantage point, it can shield the important knee joint and anchor some of the powerful leg muscles.

Femur

Patella

Tibia

Fibula

THE AMAZING OPPOSABLE THUMB

The single most important feature of the human hand is the unique "saddle joint" that lets you move your thumb from a stretched-out position all the way across your palm and "oppose" or touch each fingertip along the way.

Lacking this type of joint, your big toe is not equipped for gripping things (although it can probably pick a marble off the floor). You use its strength to push off the ground every time you take a step, and you rely on it for balance whenever you stand on "tiptoe."

ON HANDS AND FEET

Many characteristics are also shared by the hands and feet. They each have five major bones and five digits (fingers and toes), and they connect with the limbs by similar joints at the wrist and ankle.

The 8 bones of the wrist, and the 19 bones of the hand and fingers, work with the muscles in an ingenious system of levers and pincers. With this system, you can perform a remarkable variety of movements, from precise actions such as picking up a needle to broad gestures like pushing open a door.

The foot and ankle together have 26 bones, 33 joints and more than 100 ligaments (see page 48), which together support your body, keep you moving and prevent you from falling over. Designed for weight-bearing and movement, rather than for delicate actions, the foot has less flexible joints than the hand and its digits are shorter. The slight arch on the inside of the foot, with its ability to flatten out, acts as a natural, built-in shock absorber.

WHERE TWO BONES MEET:
Joint Efforts

The joints of the skeleton are the sites where two bones articulate, or come together. (Even the tiny ear bones have their own miniature joints!) *Stationary* joints, such as those between the vertebrae and between the bones of the skull, allow little or no movement. *Movable* joints, which enable the skeleton to bend and twist, are oiled by synovial fluid and held together by bands of tough, fibrous tissue called ligaments. So that two bones can move easily against each other, the weight-bearing surfaces are covered by smooth cartilage.

In addition to the saddle joint at the base of the

FEEL IT IN YOUR BONES

To see how much "play" a ball-and-socket joint allows, push your shoulders and elbows back as far as they'll go. Now bring your shoulders and arms forward to a rounded position. These movements involve the triangle-shaped scapula (shoulder bone) on each side, the clavicle (collarbone) and the humerus, which fits into the shoulder socket. Because each scapula is attached at the back only by muscle, the clavicle's job is to tie it to the sternum (breastbone) and strengthen the shoulder joint.

thumb, which allows movement up and down and from side to side, there are three major kinds of joints with varying degrees of mobility. Ball-and-socket joints, where the arms and legs connect with the body at the

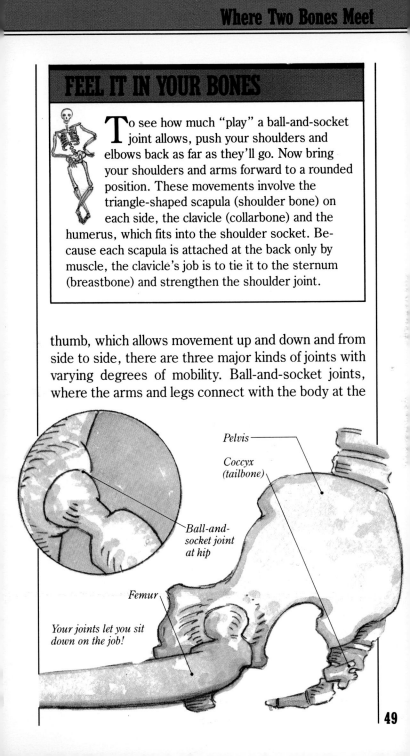

Pelvis

Coccyx
(tailbone)

Ball-and-
socket joint
at hip

Femur

*Your joints let you sit
down on the job!*

49

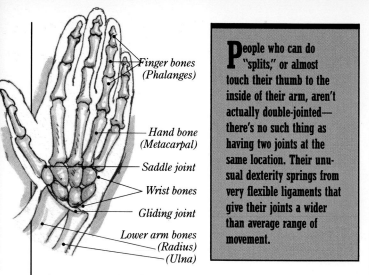

Finger bones
(Phalanges)

Hand bone
(Metacarpal)

Saddle joint

Wrist bones

Gliding joint

Lower arm bones
(Radius)
(Ulna)

People who can do "splits," or almost touch their thumb to the inside of their arm, aren't actually double-jointed—there's no such thing as having two joints at the same location. Their unusual dexterity springs from very flexible ligaments that give their joints a wider than average range of movement.

A sturdy "collar" of ligaments connects the wrist bones to the bones of the lower arm. The individual wrist bones move against each other.

shoulders and hips, permit movement in almost every direction. Hinge joints, which connect the separate arm and leg bones at the elbow and knee, work like the hinges of a door and restrict movement to one direction only.

The third major kind of joint connects the hand to the arm at the wrist, and the foot to the leg at the ankle. This gliding, or "swivel," joint allows the wrist and ankle bones to overlap and slide from side to side at the ends of the arm and leg bones, enabling the wrists and ankles to bend and rotate.

TEAMWORK

Joints not only permit movement, but also "give" under sudden pressure to absorb potential shocks to the body. When you jump down from a fence, for example, your feet flex, or bend at the toes, as you hit the ground. Your body weight then transfers back toward your heels as your arches flex—along with your ankles, knees and hip joints. Meanwhile, joints in your arms, head and back are also called upon to help you adjust your balance.

50

THE LARGEST ORGAN OF ALL:

The Skin

Your entire body is wrapped up in skin, a mostly smooth, somewhat hairy, waterproof sack that accounts for 12% of your weight.

The skin has several important jobs. In addition to making you look good, it holds in your body fluids, helps regulate your temperature, cushions and protects you, and helps defend against disease. It even forms ridges and grooves to allow your fingers and toes to get a good grip.

In the outer layer of skin, called the *epidermis*, special cells manufacture a pigment called melanin. Variations in skin color, including freckles, are caused by this pigment, as are different shades of hair color. Melanin is useful because it protects the skin from sunburn. When you spend a lot of time in the sun, granules of melanin are released and you get a tan.

The thick bottom layer of skin, the *dermis*, contains blood vessels, elastic fibers and fat. Nerve endings in the dermis send temperature, pain, touch and other sensory information to the brain.

UNINVITED GUESTS

Tiny living organisms called bacteria cover your body from head to toe. Baths and showers wash some down the drain, and perspiration carries others away, but at this very moment nearly 20 *million* "visitors" occupy every square inch on some parts of your body surface! Don't worry, though—most of them are either harmless or helpful.

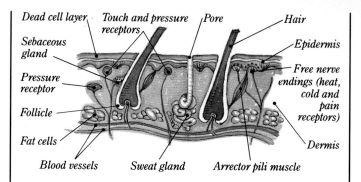

Dead cell layer · Touch and pressure receptors · Pore · Hair · Epidermis · Sebaceous gland · Pressure receptor · Free nerve endings (heat, cold and pain receptors) · Follicle · Fat cells · Dermis · Blood vessels · Sweat gland · Arrector pili muscle

Every hour, the skin has to make about one and a half million new cells just to replace all the cells that wear out in this short time span. In fact, the dead skin cells shed by the body are a major part of the dust in many homes!

HAIR-RAISERS

Did you know that hair is made mostly of dead skin cells? Only the base of each hair is alive.

Rooted in the dermis, hair grows up through the epidermis and out the pores. The skin of your scalp probably contains the roots of more than 100,000 hairs, each lasting from two to six years. The world's record for long hair is 25 feet (7.5 meters)—that's a lot of dead cells!

BODY WATCH

Strange as it seems, perspiring, or sweating, cools you off. When nerves in the skin tell the brain that your body is heating up, the brain signals the sweat glands to go to work. There are about 650 sweat glands in each square inch of skin—more than two million in all. The salty sweat they produce squirts out to the skin surface through tiny openings called *pores*. As the sweat evaporates, your skin cools off and your body temperature drops.

HARD AS NAILS

The main ingredient in your hair is keratin, a tough, fibery protein that also waterproofs and protects your skin. Calluses form on the palms of your hands and the soles of your feet when

Claws and hooves are made of keratin, too, and so are horns—but not antlers!

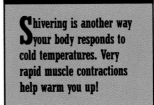

keratin accumulates to protect these areas from prolonged rubbing and pressure. This same stiffening protein is found in your nails, which are actually nothing more than specialized skin cells growing from the ends of your fingers and toes!

On a cold day, you can see how your skin and hair react to temperature. As little muscles contract around the hair follicles, the hairs straighten up. (In furry animals, this traps a layer of warm air next to the skin, but people don't have that much hair.) The muscle contraction also causes the skin to bulge up, forming

> Shivering is another way your body responds to cold temperatures. Very rapid muscle contractions help warm you up!

"goosebumps"—those tiny bumps that make the skin on your arms look like the skin of a plucked goose or chicken. Your body sometimes has the same reaction when you're really scared.

The process of aging can be noticed clearly in the skin and hair. Over the years, the skin thins out, becomes drier, and loses elasticity in the sun. Unfortunately, all your smiles, frowns and squints will end up as creases and wrinkles. What's more, the melanin supply begins to dwindle, turning your hair gray or white as its natural color "fades."

Inside the Pelvis

The pelvis, or hipbone, appears to be a single, bowl-shaped bone, but in fact it comprises six bones in all. Fused together about the time of puberty, these bones cradle the spine and important organs in the lower torso.

On each side of your body, you can feel the top, curved edge of the ilium, the largest of these bones, flaring out just below your waist. Beneath the ilium, at the front end of the pelvis, is the pubis. And at the lower back is the ischium, which forms a loop with the pubis and comes closest to touching the seat of a chair when you sit down.

THE GENDER GAP

Along with the bladder and intestines, most of the organs that account for the differences between men

FEMALE PELVIS

All three pelvic bones fuse together at the acetabulum, the cup-shaped socket where the round head of the thighbone fits.

MALE PELVIS

Ilium · Sacrum · Sperm cells · Bladder · Prostate gland · Ischium · Testis · Penis

The most obvious difference between a female skeleton and a male skeleton is in the shape of the pelvis. This helps scientists determine whether human fossil skeletons originally belonged to men or women.

and women are found inside the bowl of the pelvis.

In the female pelvis are the egg-producing ovaries and the uterus, where you began life as a fertilized egg. The male pelvis encloses the prostate gland, involved in producing and delivering the sperm that fertilize the egg. Other parts of the male reproductive system, such as the penis and testes, are outside the body.

The female pelvis is usually wider, shallower and less robust than the male pelvis, with more room between the pubic bones and sacrum. In addition, the female sacrum is shorter, wider and less curved, while the coccyx just beneath it is capable of more movement.

These gender differences in the arrangement of pelvic bones reflect the woman's child-bearing role. Her pelvis must be roomy and expandable to make childbirth possible.

SPECIAL DELIVERY

The female pelvis actually participates in child-birth! When a baby is ready to be delivered, after nine months inside the uterus, the mother's pubic bones push slightly apart at the pubic joint to widen the birth canal.

The shape of the mother's pelvis also affects the baby's position during its journey. Because the bones leave more space crosswise than from top to bottom, and the baby's head is widest from back to front, the baby turns sideways on its way through the canal to meet the outside world.

Human beings experience three big growth spurts: 1) before birth, when the fetus inside the mother increases its weight about 2.4 billion times; 2) between birth and the age of two; 3) at puberty, when young teenagers can grow 4 to 6 inches (10 to 15 centimeters) in a single year!

Fractures, Pulls, Twists and Sprains

For all its toughness and strength, the human skeleton is vulnerable to occasional fractures—or broken bones. Hit hard enough, or forced in the wrong direction, a bone can crack, splinter, or even snap in two. But thanks to its living cells, the same bone can "knit" itself back together again under a doctor's supervision.

X-ray pictures tell the doctor the exact nature of a bone break. Showing the skin and internal organs as light, misty shadows, these pictures highlight the bones and joints to reveal even "hairline" fractures.

Compact bone

Marrow

A simple fracture like this can be easily set by a doctor. A compound fracture, when the broken bone sticks out through the skin, is much more serious.

57

In the first stage of bone repair, osteoblasts bridge the fracture with fibers of collagen, which is then cemented together with mineral crystals to form new bone and a strong bond.

If the break is serious enough, the doctor will set the separate parts of bone in their proper position before applying a splint or protective cast to keep the bone from moving. Sometimes stainless-steel plates and screws are needed to hold the pieces together while the bone mends.

Bone repair is similar to the growth process. First, fibers of protein material bridge the gap between the pieces of bone to create a temporary bond. Next, the bone-making osteoblasts move into the area, grow larger, and harden it into true bone. And finally, since the site of the break can be a little lumpy with extra bone growth, special bone-destroying cells called osteoclasts dissolve away the rough edges and make the finished mend smooth.

Once mended, the break will be almost invisible, even with the help of an x-ray. And the bone will probably be as strong as it ever was!

MUSCLE AND JOINT INJURIES

In sports or other strenuous activities, injuries can occur in muscles or in the tendons that attach them to bones. Minor tears in muscle fibers happen all the time and mend themselves when the body is at rest. Muscle pulls, or stretched tendons, heal with therapy and rest. If a tendon actually pulls away from the bone, however, surgery is required to repair the injury.

Most injuries to joints occur when sudden force bends a ligament farther than it can stretch or twists it in the wrong direction. Many athletes sustain knee injuries when their weight shifts unexpectedly in a direction that the knee can't follow, wrenching the ligaments that hold the femur and tibia together. The same thing happens if you step into a hole, or off the sidewalk the wrong way, and you sprain your ankle. Applying ice and resting the injured joint is usually sufficient, although severe ligament tears may call for surgical tape and sometimes even a cast to limit movement during the healing process.

In the second stage of repair, osteoclasts move in to smooth over or destroy any rough patches of extra bone built up by the osteoblasts.

THE BIONIC HIP

A common injury among older people is a fractured hip, which usually means that the ball-shaped end of the femur has broken off. Surgeons can prevent this from happening again by replacing the ball of the femur with a much stronger metal or ceramic copy. Anchored into the good bone, the copy allows the patient to walk again.

Staying Healthy

Your skeletal structure is a marvel of design and performance, but it's only human! To stay healthy, bones and the surrounding muscles need plenty of exercise—whether it's walking to school or playing hard on a tennis or basketball court.

Physical activity strengthens the bones, flexes the muscles, and keeps the joints in good working order. Running and swimming, in particular, bring fresh blood and oxygen to the cells by giving the heart and lungs a thorough workout. Bicycling and exercises such as sit-ups and push-ups, which build up the big muscles of the torso, arms and legs, benefit your skeleton by improving posture.

Warming up beforehand with slow, steady stretches is important for muscles and tendons. Whatever the activity, begin slowly and gradually step up the pace to increase your heart rate. Too much, too soon, and you risk tearing a muscle or putting a strain on your heart.

After exercising, you need to cool down, relax, and stretch the muscles out again. Stretching helps keep your body flexible, enjoying a full range of movement in the limbs, neck and back.

FUELING UP

Bones and muscles stay in good shape through exercise, but they also need fuel for energy. People have been known to survive as long as 10 days with no water, and two and a half months with no food, but not without tremendous harm to their body tissues.

As a growing child, building a skeleton for life, you should pay special attention to diet. Particularly good for bones are foods like broccoli and milk, which are rich in calcium and phosphorus. As long as you eat a balanced diet, however, you'll feed your bones all the minerals and vitamins they need and still have enough left over to fuel the rest of your body—with energy to spare.

Some features of your bone and muscle structure are inherited from your parents, but a lot depends on you—especially now, while you're still growing.

The Way We Were . . .

The human body has gone through many changes over the years. Fossil remains of the earliest humans and their ancestors tell us that our frames are more slender and less muscular than theirs, and that we stand taller and straighter than they did. Early humans were generally more rugged-looking, with a lot more hair, bony ridges over their eyes, and jaws that jutted forward to hold their large teeth.

You might be better at baseball or operating a computer, but out in the woods your distant ancestor could do a better job of hunting and gathering food for dinner.

A fossil nicknamed Lucy, found in Ethiopia, told us a lot about what we once looked like. From the skeletal bones, dating back 3.5 million years, scientists concluded that Lucy was probably a human ancestor. The shape of her pelvis showed that she was a woman and that she walked nearly upright.

The pelvis reflects a crucial change in the human skeleton. Unlike the pelvis of a creature who walks on all fours, ours has assumed a rounded, upright shape that lines up the legs with the spine and enables us to stand erect. This posture allows the legs to carry our weight and frees the hands for other work.

The shape of the cranium has also changed to accommodate a larger brain. Early human skulls were lower in the forehead and longer at the back, indicating that the front of the brain—where intelligence, thought, memory and sensory interpretations are centered—was less developed than ours. Physical coordination and automatic responses, controlled by the cerebellum at the back of the skull, were far more important millions of years ago.

WHERE DO WE GO FROM HERE?

Assuming that most changes in our structure will continue in the same direction, we can try to predict the shape of things to come. We might consider body parts that seem to have either less or greater significance as times goes on. The brain, for example, seems to be increasingly important, but what about wisdom teeth and the little toe? Some organs, like the tonsils and appendix, seem to be extra—at least, we know the body can get along without them.

Changes in our appearance might include an even bigger cranium and enormous eyes in a smaller face. Although computers are getting smarter all the time, they'll never replace the human brain. The frontal lobes, above and behind the eyes, may need more

What do you think? Would you be able to see the family resemblance 100,000 years from now (4,000 generations in the future) in your great-great-great- . . . great-grandson or granddaughter?

room with corresponding changes in the shape of the skull. Since we'll probably depend even more on our eyes, especially for reading, we can expect these sensory organs to increase in size. Noses, on the other hand, are likely to grow smaller as their original function of sniffing out danger becomes obsolete. There may be less need for chewing, since more and more foods will be processed, so our teeth may get smaller and fewer in number.

Females in the future might have big heads *and* big hips, because the birth process will require a wider, more expandable pelvis.

With less physical work demanded of us, our frames will probably continue to grow more slender while our muscles get smaller. If harm to the environment reduces food production, thin people will have an advantage because they'll need less to eat. Pollution and damage to the ozone layer may give rise to harder, tougher skin to resist fumes, acid rain and snow, and ultraviolet radiation.

Will fingers get longer? Will we have as many toes? Your thoughts and predictions are just as valuable as those of the scientists and science-fiction writers who think about these matters. One thing is certain. All life-forms change, however slowly, and someday our skeleton will have a new look!